THE POCKET

POCKET

IMPRESSIONISM

Published in 2025
by Gemini Gift Books
Part of Gemini Books Group

Based in Woodbridge and London

Marine House, Tide Mill Way,
Woodbridge, Suffolk IP12 1AP
United Kingdom

www.geminibooks.com

Text and Design © 2025 Gemini Gift Books Ltd
Part of the Gemini Pockets series

Cover illustration by Natalie Foss
Text by Roland Hall

ISBN 978-1-80247-326-1

A CIP catalogue record for this book is available from the British Library.

Manufacturer's EU Representative: Eurolink Compliance Limited, 25 Herbert Place,
Dublin, D02 AY86, Republic of Ireland. admin@eurolink-europe.ie

Printed in China

10 9 8 7 6 5 4 3 2 1

MIX
Paper | Supporting
responsible forestry
FSC® C117745

Picture credits: Alamy Stock Photo: Archivart 4; World History Archive 8; Chronicle
30; 42; Steve Vidler 40-41; Classic Image 54; Harold Watercress 58; The History
Collection 62; Everett Collection Historical 68, 72; Ian Dagnall Computing 74, 94;
Archive PL 78, 82; The Picture Art Collection 84; Science History Images 104;
steeve-x-art 106-7, 110; Folio 120. Getty Images: Pobytov 10, 19, 22-23, 27, 56-57, 61,
64-65, 86, 91, 92, 112-3, 115, 119; kampee patisena 12, 13; Eglelip 14; Kittipong Chararoj
17; Heritage Images 20; Dan Totilca 32, 36; oxygen 45, 47, 50-51; lynnebeclu 76-77;
PhotoStock-Israel 97, 99, 103; Zhanna Danilova 122, 125.

THE
POCKET

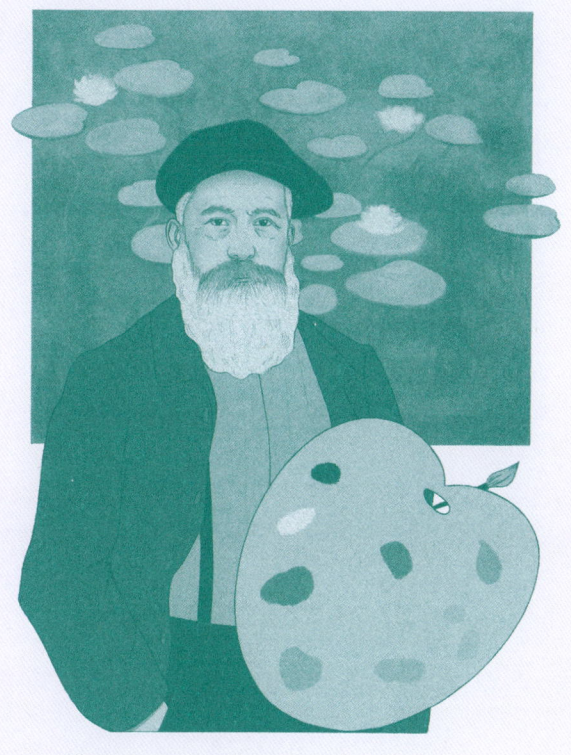

IMPRESSIONISM

G:

CONTENTS

INTRODUCTION

Impressionism evolved in the late nineteenth century in France. It was born when artists started to paint an "impression" of what they saw rather than a faithful, realistic reproduction of the subject matter. An emphasis on vibrant colours, loose brushwork and a focus on light and atmosphere made it very different from what had come before.

It is now one of the most popular art movements in the world, and famous works are viewed by admirers in huge numbers. Claude Monet's house in Giverny, France, is visited by half a million people every year. But it was not always the case, for the early Impressionist painters were mocked by the artistic establishment.

This is the story of Impressionism and ten of its most famous artists.

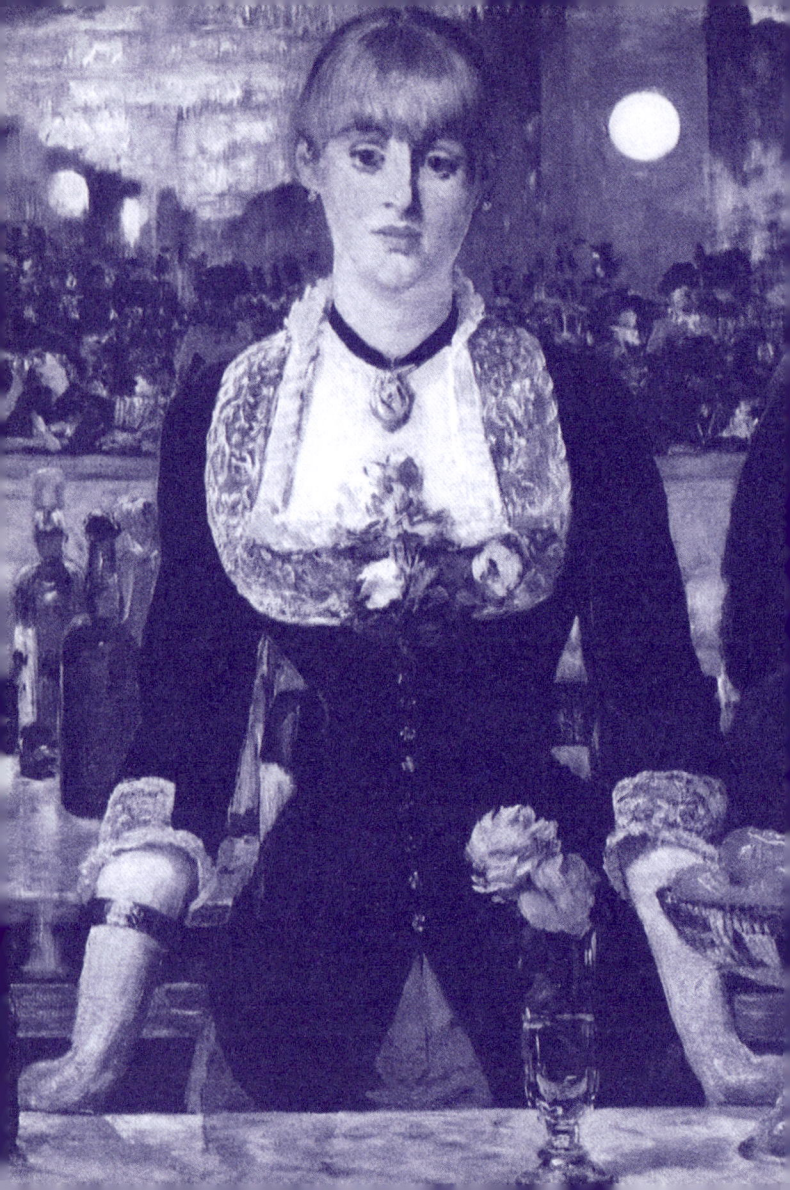

ORIGINS & INFLUENCES

WHAT IS IMPRESSIONISM?

The story of Impressionism begins in the 1860s in Paris, when Claude Monet and a number of other Paris-based painters began to work in a similar style, with a common outlook. They painted outside, quickly, rather than working from sketches in a studio. They were interested in light and colour and how it was recorded on the canvas. They shared common themes, too: water and sky in landscapes, as well as everyday street scenes and people.

The key was that the artists painted not necessarily what was in front of them; it was the *impression* of what they saw, rather than a faithful, photographic-like reproduction of the landscape, that was important to their personal vision. It was a new approach, and it changed the history of art forever.

ORIGINS

Artists had been painting landscapes in open spaces for many years. British landscape artist John Constable (1776–1837) was a pioneer of this method of working, in the early nineteenth century. However, painting in a spontaneous fashion was almost unheard of, and freer brush strokes even more so.

Certainly artists Eugene Delacroix (1798–1863) and J.M.W. Turner (1775–1851), with their loose painterly style, would have had great influence on the Impressionists.

FIRST EXHIBITION

The main protagonist of Impressionism was Monet, but he was just one of a group of artists who were painting in this new style. Jean Renoir, Edgar Degas, Paul Cézanne and Monet mounted what was the first group exhibition of Impressionists, in 1874 in Paris.

It was an abject failure. Critics treated the paintings with derision, because the style was so different from traditional painting methods. The artists were ridiculed, and the term Impressionism used as an insult.

IMPRESSION, SUNRISE

BY CLAUDE MONET, 1872

Location: Musée Marmottan Monet, Paris, France

This is the work that gave the movement its name. Freed from the constraints of the studio, Monet committed to canvas the impression of what was in front of him: blurry reflections, splinters of light on water and murky shadows in the distance. The painting changed the face of art forever.

BOULEVARD MONTMARTRE À PARIS

BY CAMILLE PISSARRO, 1897

Location: Metropolitan Museum of Art, New York, USA

This is a view of a busy Parisian street. It is an example of one of the everyday scenes of modern life that were painted by the Impressionists. Other examples included parks, cafés and riverside scenes.

Dark, textured and vibrant, the style matches the content, and the city almost seems to move.

DIFFERENT

Contemporary art at the time tended to favour religious or Classical subject matter and carefully reproduced imagery. The Parisian art establishment was centred around the Salon, an annual exhibition, for which art was selected by the prestigious Académie des Beaux-Arts in Paris.

Impressionist painters, with their loose brushwork, colourful shadows and ordinary subjects were not favoured by the Salon.

EVOLUTION

Seven further group exhibitions took place after 1874, and the movement expanded. More artists were involved, including Berthe Morisot and Édouard Manet, and Impressionism became more popular with critics and the public alike.

Camille Pissarro was the only artist to feature his work in all eight of those displays, and by the time of the last one, 1886, the most established Impressionists such as Monet and Renoir were famous enough to have their own solo exhibitions.

LUNCHEON OF THE BOATING PARTY

BY PIERRE-AUGUSTE RENOIR, 1881

Location: The Phillips Collection, Washington, DC, USA

A fascinating combination of still life and landscape, this was painted by Renoir near a river not far from Paris. A slice of nineteenth-century life, it features the painter Gustave Caillebotte at the bottom right, and Renoir's future wife, Aline Charigot, opposite him. It is a fine example of the Impressionist treatment of light, brushstroke and subject matter.

UNITY

Impressionist artists were initially united in three main ways. First, in the style of their work, which tended to be free and colourful. Second, they had a personal instead of conventional approach to their subject matter. Third, they had a desire to find what they judged to be a true reproduction of nature.

But as a group, the Impressionists had started to dissolve from the early 1880s. Individual painters developed their own styles or focussed on different principles. For example, Paul Cézanne became famous as a Post-Impressionist, and, Paul Gaugin evolved from Impressionism towards Symbolist art.

LASTING INFLUENCE

Impressionism was an extremely influential style, and could be described as the first "modern" art movement in that it reflected contemporary culture and understanding. Neo-Impressionism and Post-Impressionism followed, both of which further developed the use of colour and free brushwork.

Other significant movements that were influenced by Impressionism were Cubism (abstract imagery) and Fauvism (wild brushwork and colours).

Impressionism is even an influence on Pop Art, where the capture of a fleeting moment, the transient nature of light and everyday scenes make up important elements.

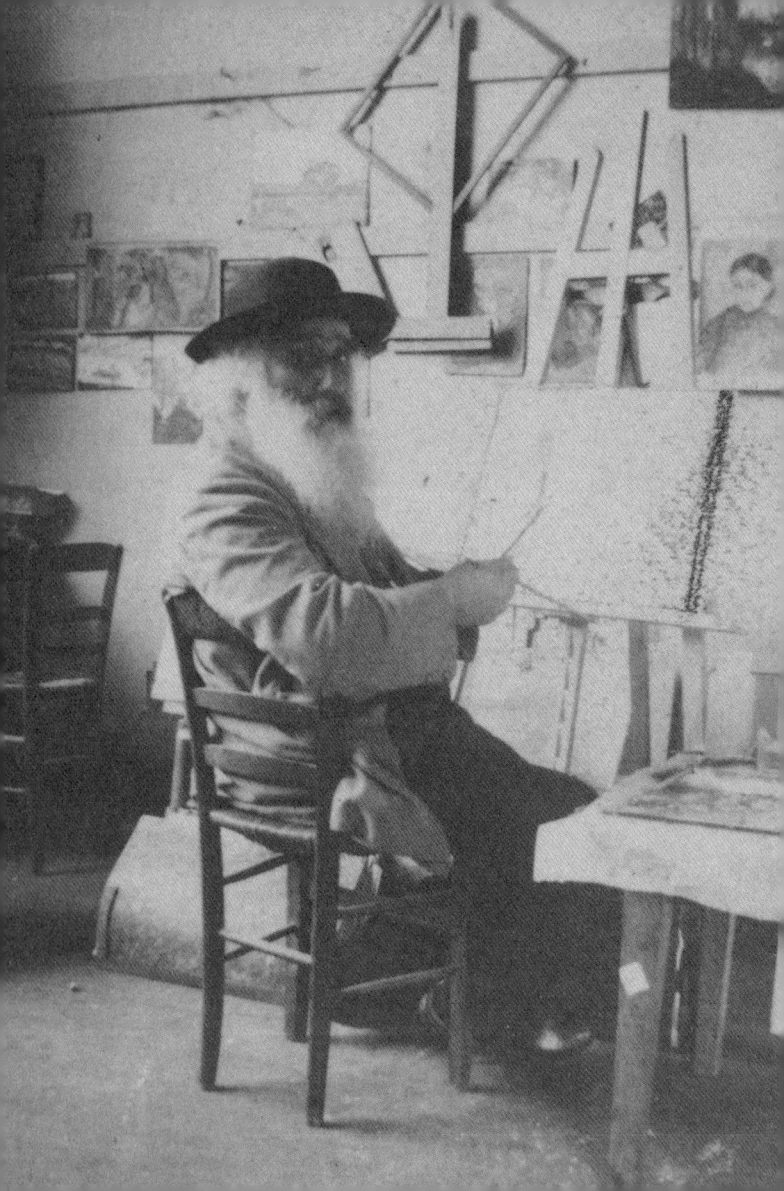

CAMILLE PISSARRO

1830–1903

Place of birth/death:

Saint Thomas, Danish West Indies/
Paris, France

Key works:

Jalais Hill, Pontoise (1867)
*Jardin et poulailler chez Octave Mirbeau,
Les Damps* (1892)
The Boulevard Montmartre at Night (1897)
The Seine and the Louvre (1903)

EARLY YEARS

Jacob Abraham Camille Pissarro
was born on the island of St. Thomas
(now part of the U.S. Virgin Islands,
at the time part of Denmark) in
1830. He lived there until he was 12,
when he was sent to boarding school
in France (his parents were both
of French heritage), and where he
developed a love of art and drawing.

He returned to St. Thomas in 1847
and lived there and in Venezuela until
1855, when he moved to Paris.

EVOLUTION AND STYLE

Pissarro was pivotal to the Impressionist movement that developed in Paris. He was older than the other members, and a gentle, inspirational influence.

However, his work was Impressionist in style and content, and it drew attention. Pissarro was particularly well known for his portrayals of ordinary people in natural settings, for example *Peasant Girl Drinking her Coffee* (1881) and *Haymaking, Éragny* (1887).

"I began to understand my sensations, to know what I wanted, at around the age of forty."

CAMILLE PISSARRO,
PAINTING OUTSIDE THE LINES: PATTERNS OF CREATIVITY IN MODERN ART BY DAVID W. GALENSON, 2001

SUCCESS

After spending time in London during the Franco-Prussian War (1870–71), Pissarro returned to France, where he continued to work and exhibit.

Pissarro was the only artist to have shown his work at all eight Paris Impressionist exhibitions, between 1874 and 1886.

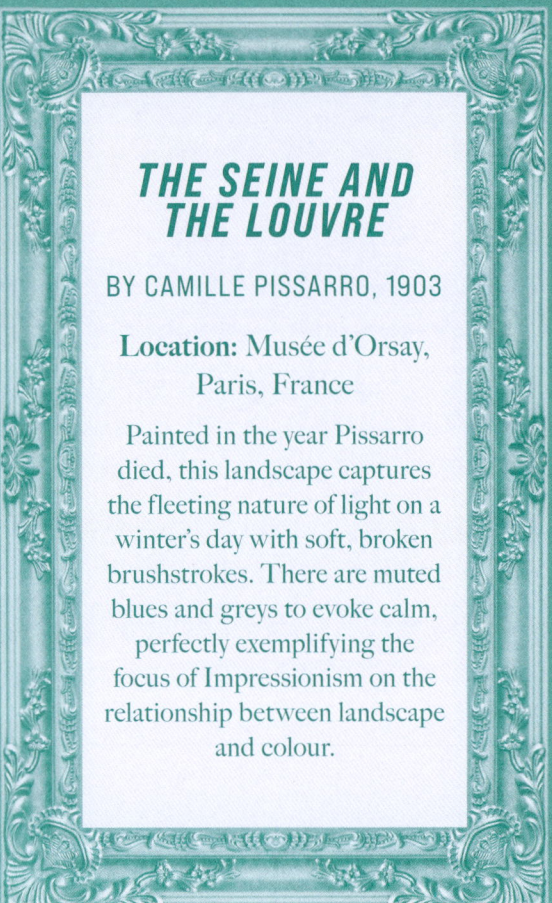

THE SEINE AND THE LOUVRE

BY CAMILLE PISSARRO, 1903

Location: Musée d'Orsay, Paris, France

Painted in the year Pissarro died, this landscape captures the fleeting nature of light on a winter's day with soft, broken brushstrokes. There are muted blues and greys to evoke calm, perfectly exemplifying the focus of Impressionism on the relationship between landscape and colour.

"It is only by drawing often, drawing everything, drawing incessantly, that one fine day you discover to your surprise that you have rendered something in its true character."

CAMILLE PISSARRO,
CAMILLE PISSARRO: LETTERS TO HIS SON LUCIEN, 1943

"Everything is beautiful, all that matters is to be able to interpret."

CAMILLE PISSARRO,
*LETTERS OF THE GREAT ARTISTS
– FROM BLAKE TO POLLOCK* BY
RICHARD FRIEDENTHAL, 1963

LEGACY

Pissarro was important to many artists, not only Impressionists. He was a mentor to Paul Cézanne, he guided Paul Gauguin early in his career, and he supported the Neo-Impressionist artists Georges Seurat (1859–91) and Paul Signac (1863–1935).

This means Pissarro was influential in the subsequent movements of Cubism, Fauvism and even Abstract Expressionism.

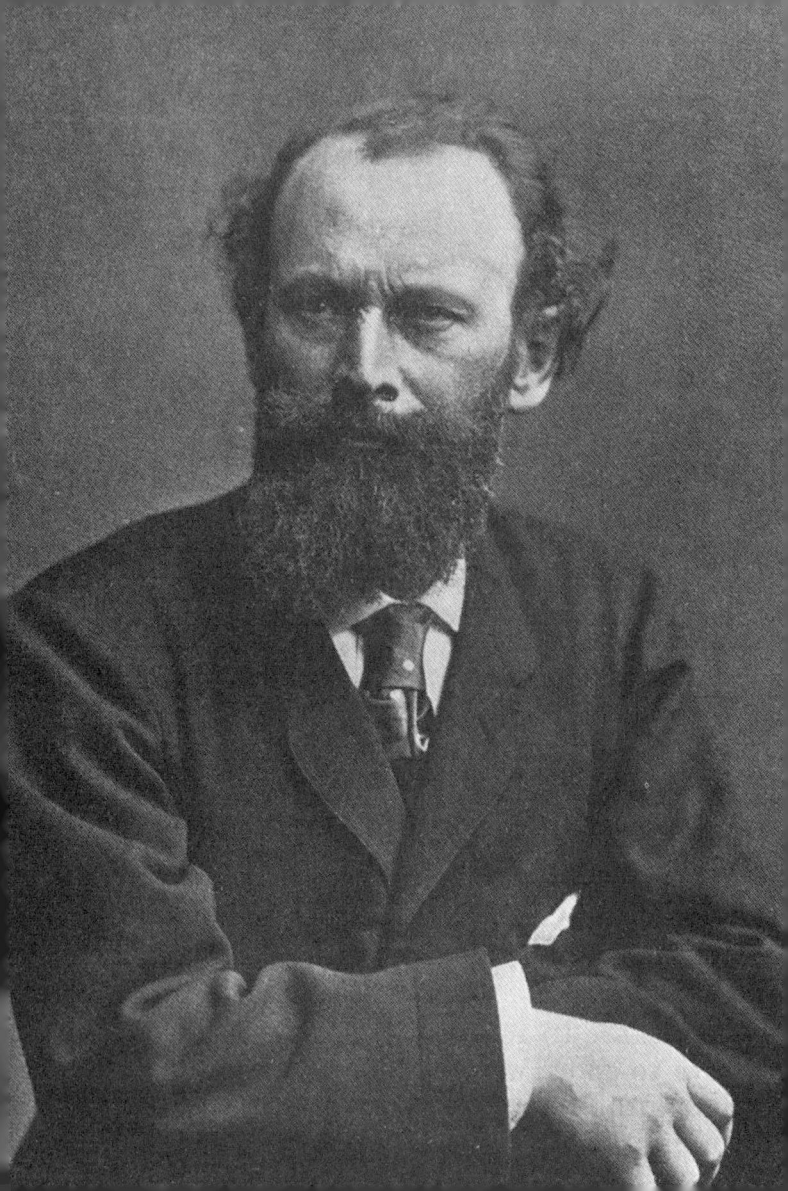

ÉDOUARD MANET

1832–1883

Place of birth/death:

Paris, France/Paris, France

Key works:

The Luncheon on the Grass (1863)
Olympia (1863–65)
Bullfight (1865–66)
Spring (1881)
A Bar at the Folies-Bergère (1882)

EARLY YEARS

Similarly to many of the other Impressionist artists, Édouard Manet was born in Paris to an affluent family. His mother was the daughter of a diplomat and his father was a judge. As the oldest son, Édouard was expected to follow a career in law. However, he tried to join the navy but failed the entrance exams, then turned to his real passion, art, in order to study. He spent much time admiring the paintings in the Louvre museum.

"I don't know
why I'm here.
Everything
before our eyes
is ridiculous."

ÉDOUARD MANET,
MANET BY NATHALIA BRODSKAYA, 2011

LEARNING

Manet became a pupil of the artist Thomas Couture, and by the time he was 24 he had his own studio. Before the Impressionist movement was founded, Manet was labelled a "realist" painter. His subject matter was ordinary people, contrary to the popular artistic conventions at the time, and he was able to make an income from his art.

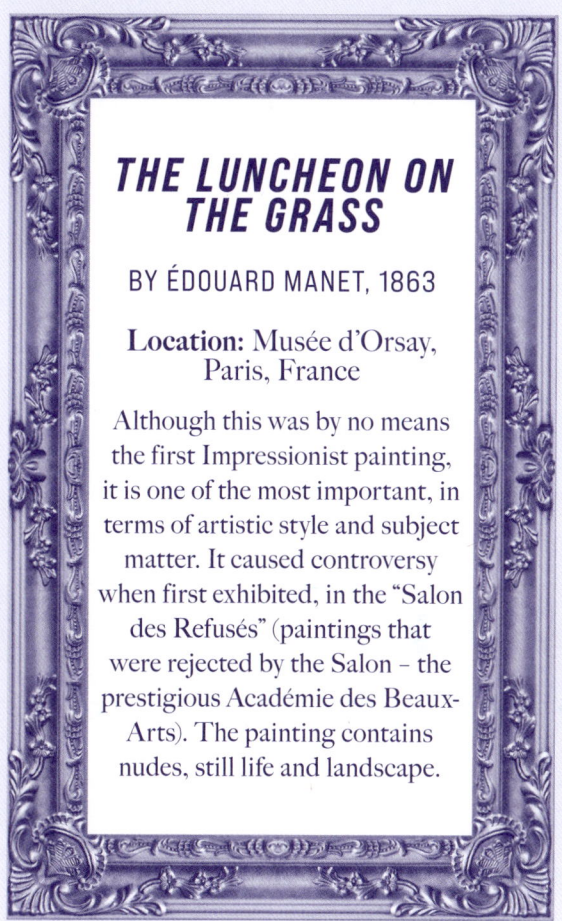

THE LUNCHEON ON THE GRASS

BY ÉDOUARD MANET, 1863

Location: Musée d'Orsay, Paris, France

Although this was by no means the first Impressionist painting, it is one of the most important, in terms of artistic style and subject matter. It caused controversy when first exhibited, in the "Salon des Refusés" (paintings that were rejected by the Salon – the prestigious Académie des Beaux-Arts). The painting contains nudes, still life and landscape.

MODERN LIFE

An enduring theme of Manet's paintings is the outdoor life of Parisians. This is one of the reasons he is seen as emblematic of the whole Impressionist movement. He depicted large scenes of social gatherings in the French capital, and *Music in the Tuileries* (1862) is a prime example.

In the Impressionist group of artists, Manet formed a particular friendship with Berthe Morisot, who later married his brother Eugène.

ÉDOUARD MANET

"He has no talent at all, that boy... tell him please to give up painting."

ÉDOUARD MANET ON PIERRE-AUGUSTE RENOIR,
THE HISTORY OF IMPRESSIONISM
BY JOHN REWALD, 1961

"In the figure, look for the main light and the main shadow, the rest will come of itself: often, it amounts to very little."

ÉDOUARD MANET,
THE ART HISTORY ARCHIVE, 2001

STYLE

Manet's work was founded on the opposition of light and shadow. The colour palette he used was quite restricted, especially for an Impressionist, and black was an important feature of his work.

He associated with avant-garde writers such as Charles Baudelaire (1821–67), and chose his frequently unconventional subject matter from many levels of Parisian life. He chose to feature ordinary people who would not normally be the subject of paintings.

LATER YEARS

In the 1870s, under the influence of Monet and Renoir, Manet produced landscapes and street scenes that were inspired by the principles of Impressionism.

However, he still remained reluctant to exhibit and ally himself with the Impressionists.

He died in 1883, only 51 years old.

Manet's *Spring*, painted in 1881, sold for $65 million to the J. Paul Getty Museum in Los Angeles in 2014. It was the most expensive sale of the artist's work to date.

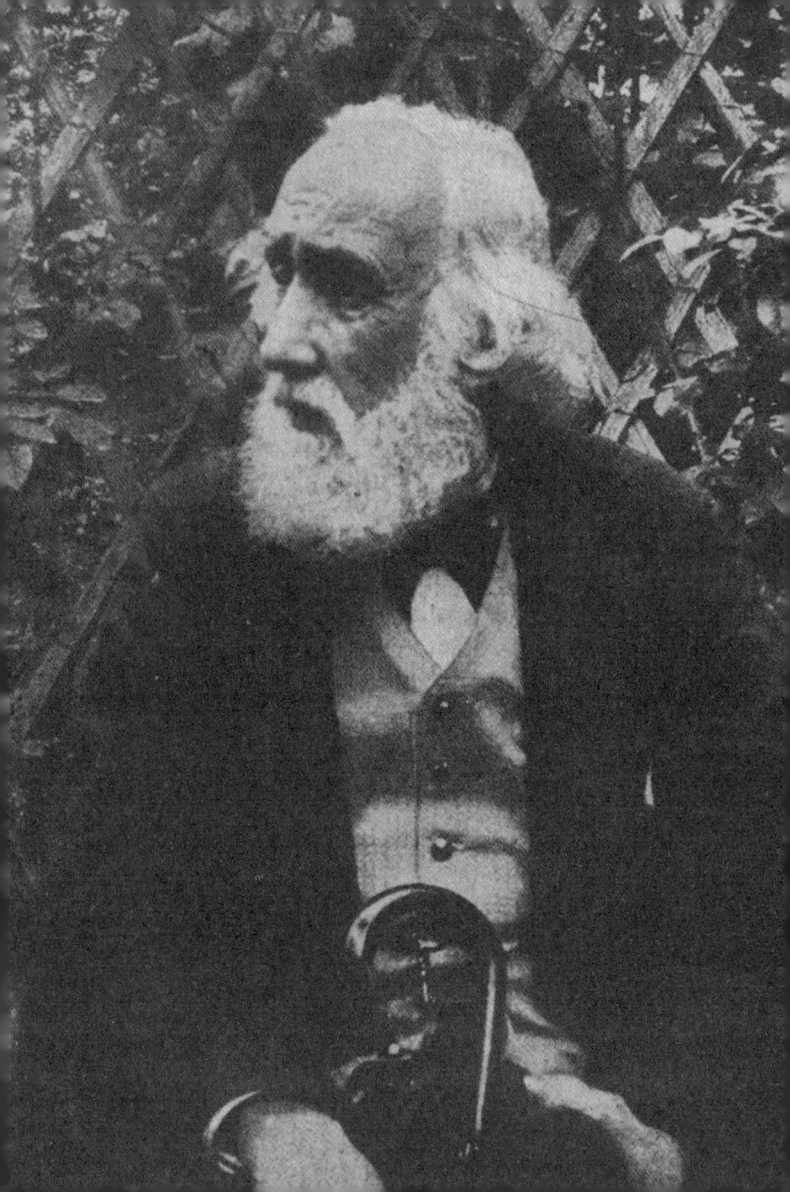

EDGAR DEGAS

1834–1917

Place of birth/death:

Paris, France/Paris, France

Key works:

Musicians in the Orchestra (1872)
The Dance Class (1874)
The Absinthe Drinker (1875)
Dancers Practicing at the Barre (1877)

EARLY YEARS

Edgar Degas was born in Paris in 1834, under the birth name of Hilaire-Germain-Edgar De Gas. He came from a wealthy family, his father a banker. He developed a love of art from an early age, and by the time he was 18 he had a studio in the family home. His father wanted him to study law and he enrolled to do so, but he did not pursue it for long and was admitted to the prestigious École des Beaux-Arts in Paris in 1855.

"Only when he no longer knows what he is doing does the painter do good things."

EDGAR DEGAS,
DENVER ART MUSEUM, 2018

"Boredom soon overcomes me when I am contemplating nature."

EDGAR DEGAS,
*THE NOTEBOOKS OF
EDGAR DEGAS*, 1976

ITALIAN INSPIRATION

After only a year at art school, Degas travelled to Italy, where he ended up staying for three years. It was here that he made the initial studies for one of his famous early masterpieces, *The Bellelli Family* (1873), and he showed an interest in Italian Renaissance painters: Michelangelo and Titian in particular.

REALISTIC APPROACH

Although a very important painter – and one of the founders – of the Impressionist movement, Degas did not like the term, preferring to call himself a "realist".

He worked a lot with sculpture, drawing and prints. He even used the rapidly emerging, modern medium of photography.

Degas' favourite subject was dancers and more than half of all his work was dedicated to them; most of his works were created inside or in the studio.

"It is all well and good to copy what one sees, but it is much better to draw only what remains in one's memory."

EDGAR DEGAS,
*THE ANNENBERG COLLECTION:
MASTERPIECES OF IMPRESSIONISM
AND POST-IMPRESSIONISM, 2003*

ESTABLISHED STYLE

When he returned from Italy, Degas settled in Paris with a new studio, but on the outbreak of the Franco–Prussian War he volunteered and served in the National Guard. There he learned of his defective eyesight; he would worry about his vision for the rest of his life.

After the war he visited family in New Orleans, where he painted various pieces, including the well-known *A Cotton Office in New Orleans.*

By 1874 he was back in Paris, painting for a living. He was an established part of the Impressionist movement by now, despite his apparent disdain for some aspects of it.

"An artist is
a deception...
an artist is
only an artist
at certain
times."

EDGAR DEGAS,
*BERTHE MORISOT, THE FIRST
LADY OF IMPRESSIONISM*
BY MARGARET SHENNAN, 1996

SUSTAINED SUCCESS

Degas made a good living from his artistic work, and he also amassed a significant art collection by purchasing works from other artists. He bought pieces from fellow Impressionists but also collected works by Paul Gauguin, Vincent Van Gogh and Eugène Delacroix, among others.

By 1890 his eyesight prevented him from painting, although he continued to work in other mediums.

THE DANCE CLASS

BY EDGAR DEGAS, 1874

Location: Musée d'Orsay, Paris, France

This is a large, ambitious work by Degas, containing more than 20 dancers, observers and a ballet master, Jules Perrot.

It is significant for its treatment of light and colour, with a soft interior light that was different from many other Impressionists. The brushwork is also more structured, demonstrating Degas' distinctive individual style.

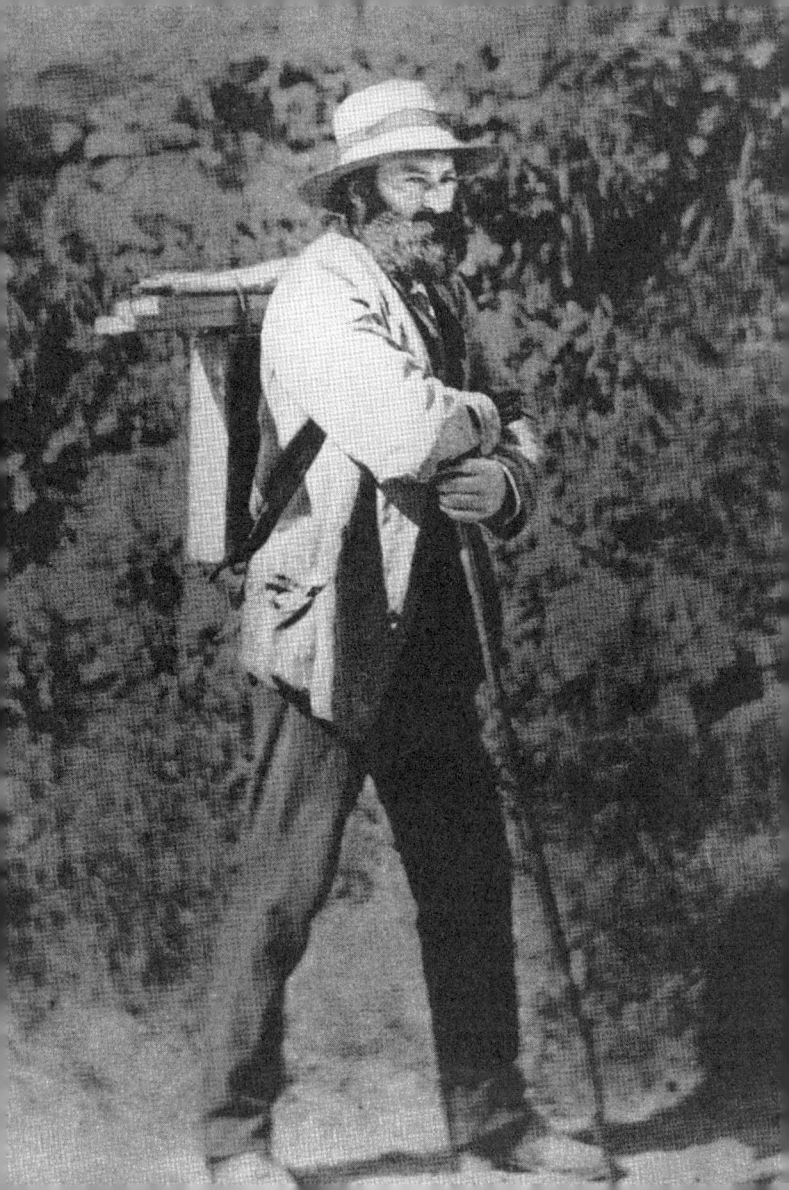

PAUL CÉZANNE

1839–1906

Place of birth/death:

Aix-en-Provence, France/
Aix-en-Provence, France

Key works:

The Hanged Man's House (1873)
Madame Cézanne in a Red Armchair (c. 1877)
The Bay of Marseilles, Seen from L'Estaque (c. 1885)
The Basket of Apples (c. 1893)

EARLY YEARS

Paul Cézanne was born in Aix-en-Provence, France, in 1839. His father was wealthy and became the head of a bank, ensuring financial stability for the family. After school, Cézanne went to law school as his father wanted him to, but he found more pleasure in painting and writing poetry (he was childhood friends with the writer Émile Zola). After two years he decided to go to Paris to pursue his dream of becoming an artist. He had already been studying drawing at night school and felt that he had found his calling.

"Art is a harmony parallel with nature."

PAUL CÉZANNE,
PAULCEZANNE.ORG

DREAMS OF PARIS

In Paris, Cézanne's paintings were turned down for the Salon of the École des Beaux-Arts.

However, he continued to pursue his own, less formal style of painting and after his "dark period" in the 1860s, his work became more Impressionist in style. In 1874 he exhibited with the Impressionists in Paris.

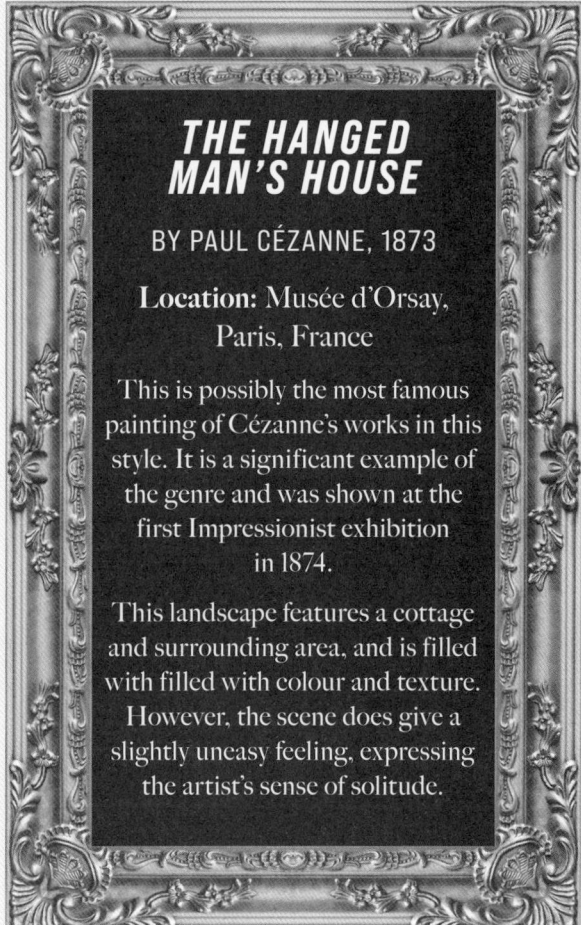

THE HANGED MAN'S HOUSE

BY PAUL CÉZANNE, 1873

Location: Musée d'Orsay, Paris, France

This is possibly the most famous painting of Cézanne's works in this style. It is a significant example of the genre and was shown at the first Impressionist exhibition in 1874.

This landscape features a cottage and surrounding area, and is filled with filled with colour and texture. However, the scene does give a slightly uneasy feeling, expressing the artist's sense of solitude.

MAKING AN IMPRESSION

Cézanne made friends with Camille Pissarro and, being older, became his mentor. Cézanne fitted in with the Impressionists, and his choice of subjects and use of colour reflected the influence of those other artists. But by 1878, Cézanne moved on and his style developed.

He is now most famously remembered as a Post-Impressionist, and his work also overlapped into Cubism. Whatever the label, Cézanne is without a doubt one of the most important painters of his era.

SUCCESS

Cézanne's work has sold consistently – even during his lifetime. One of the most expensive paintings of all time was one of his versions of *The Card Players* (1894–95). It sold for $250 million in 2011 and held the record for the highest price ever paid for a painting, until 2017.

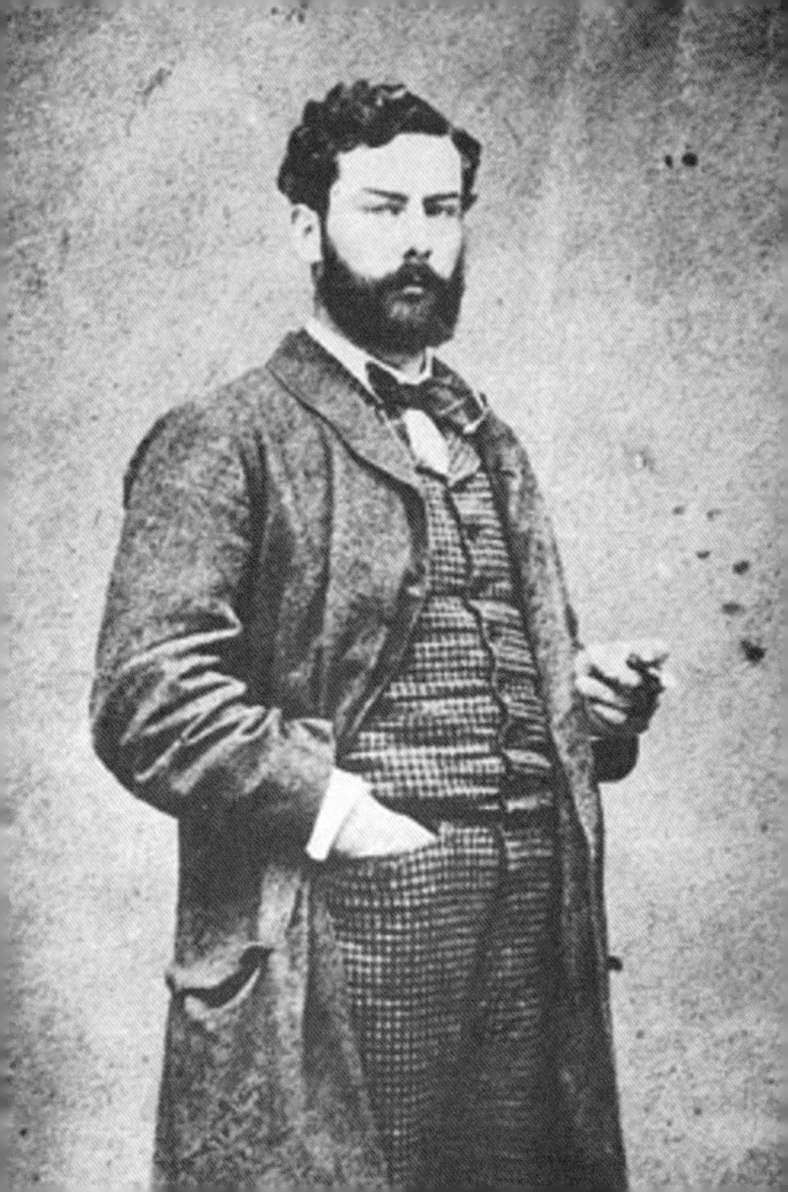

ALFRED SISLEY

1839–1899

Place of birth/death:

Paris, France/Moret-sur-Loing, France

Key works:

View of the Canal Saint-Martin (1870)
Boulevard Héloïse, Argenteuil (1872)
Flood at Port Marly (1872)
Snow in Louveciennes (1878)

EARLY YEARS

Alfred Sisley was born in Paris in 1839 to British parents who lived and worked in the city.

Although Sisley chose to live most of his life in France, he became interested in painting during his studies in London, where he saw the work of British artists such as John Constable and J.M.W. Turner.

OPEN AIR

Sisley spent four years in London before returning to Paris, where, as many other Impressionists, he studied under the tutelage of the Swiss artist Charles Gleyre. It was here that he met Claude Monet, Pierre-Auguste Renoir and Frédéric Bazille. Together the young painters would travel outside Paris, and paint landscapes in the open air.

TECHNICAL INNOVATION

One of the reasons the Impressionists were able to paint spontaneously outside was the new technical innovation of premixed paint that was easily available in small tubes. Prior to this, an artist (or their assistant) would have to spend a lot of time mixing paint in preparation for a day's work.

"Sisley was an atmosphere guy, and like almost all his colleagues, he painted *en plein air*, taking his canvas and palette to the banks of the Seine or to towns west of Paris."

JASON FARAGO,
THE NEW YORK TIMES, 2017

RECOGNITION

Despite his commitment to the Impressionist style, and the acknowledged high quality of his output, Sisley's works never received the same recognition as those of his Impressionist colleagues. Even when he exhibited paintings in the Salon, Sisley struggled to make a living from his work; instead he had to rely on patronage. Sisley spent most of his life poor, and it was not until after his death at the end of the nineteenth century that his paintings began to increase in popularity and value.

OEUVRE

Sisley produced nearly 1,000 pieces, the vast majority of them oil paintings, the others pastels and drawings. His most favoured subject matter was landscapes, and it is for them that he is most famously remembered. Although he lived most of his life in France and painted the majority of his works there, Sisley visited England frequently and liked to paint the countryside, in particular in and around London. One key example of this is *View of the Thames: Charing Cross Bridge* (1874).

"Sisley has a good eye, and his work will certainly charm all those whose artistic sense is not very refined."

CAMILLE PISSARRO ON SISLEY,
CAMILLE PISSARRO – LETTERS TO HIS SON LUCIEN, 1943

BOULEVARD HÉLOÏSE, ARGENTEUIL

BY ALFRED SISLEY, 1872

Location: National Gallery of Art, Washington, DC, USA

Sisley was not the only Impressionist to paint this street scene – Monet did too – but Sisley's is a fine example of his early work. Sombre shades abound and a plethora of browns are masterfully adapted to give the painting great depth.

This work embodies all the Impressionists' ideas.

FINAL YEARS

Unlike most of his colleagues, Sisley never strayed from the path of Impressionism. He continued to paint the landscapes he so favoured, and his oeuvre is filled with them. In 1898 Sisley applied for French citizenship but it was never granted to him and he died, as an Englishman abroad, in 1899.

"His paintings simply explore the way we see – and, I realise... we see in the same way, whether you happen to be in Wales or France."

JONATHAN JONES ON SISLEY,
THE GUARDIAN, 2008

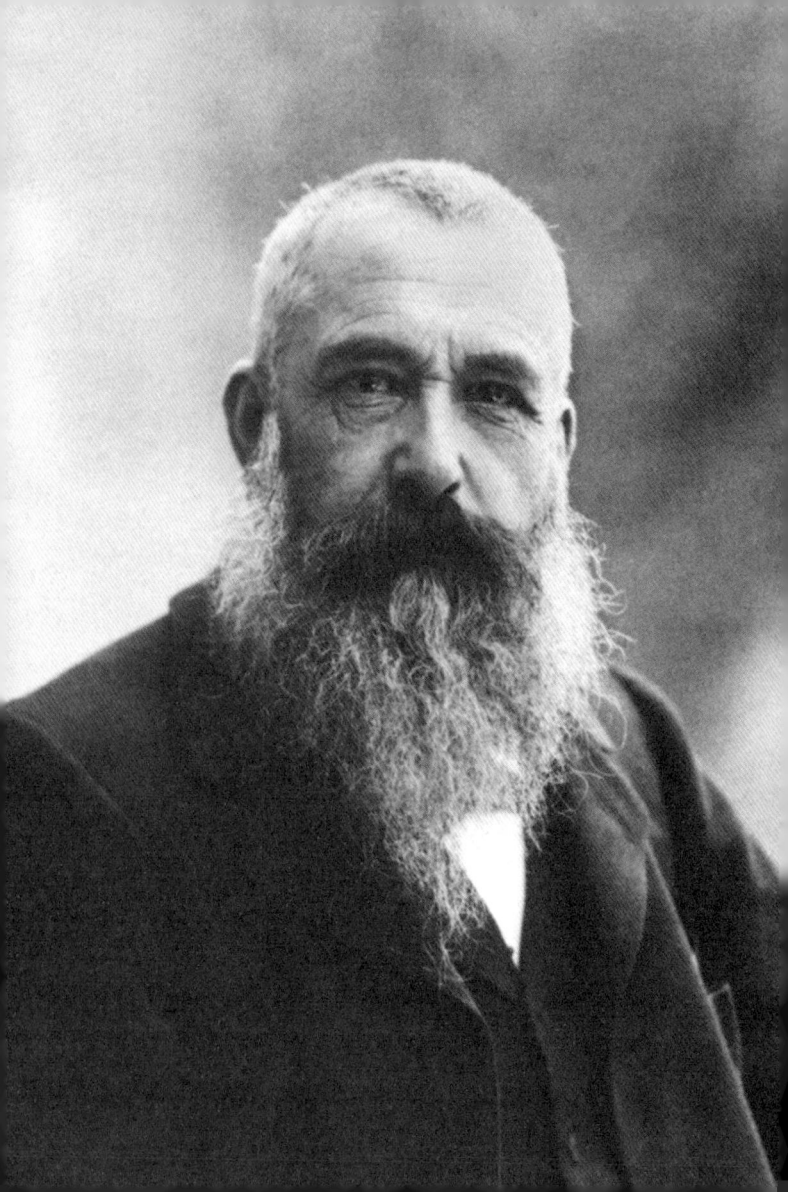

CLAUDE MONET

1840–1926

Place of birth/death:

Paris, France/Giverny, France

Key works:

Impression, Sunrise (1872)
The Water-lily pond (1899)
Rouen Cathedral (series 1892–94)
The Houses of Parliament, Sunset (1902)

EARLY YEARS

Claude Monet was born in Paris in 1840. Five years later the family moved to Le Havre in Normandy, on France's northern coast.

As a young man at school, Monet met the landscape painter Eugène Boudin (1824–98), who encouraged him to paint and accompanied him on trips to paint *en plein air* (open air) in the local area.

In 1859 he moved to Paris to continue his formal artistic training at the avant-garde Académie Suisse.

"I hope to produce masterpieces, because I like the countryside very much."

CLAUDE MONET,
*MONET'S YEARS AT GIVERNY:
BEYOND IMPRESSIONISM*
BY DANIEL WILDENSTEIN, 1978

"I am in a very
black mood
and profoundly
disgusted with
painting. It really is a
continual torture!"

CLAUDE MONET,
*LETTERS OF THE GREAT ARTISTS
– FROM BLAKE TO POLLOCK*
BY RICHARD FRIEDENTHAL, 1963

THE WATER-LILY POND

BY CLAUDE MONET, 1899

Location: Pola Museum of Art, Kanagawa, Japan

Monet painted around 250 images of what was probably his favourite subject: water-lilies. Most of them were studies in the garden at his home in Giverny. This painting, *W.1511*, is a beautiful example of the build-up of colour, texture and shade for which much of the series is so famous.

ESTABLISHMENT

Monet entered the studio of Charles Gleyre in Paris in 1862, where he met Pierre-Auguste Renoir and Alfred Sisley.

He became the leading French Impressionist landscape painter and exhibited in most of the group's exhibitions. His 1872 painting *Impression, Sunrise*, (see page 13), was called an "impression", not a finished painting, by critic Louis Leroy.

GIVERNY

After travelling in the 1880s, Monet acquired a property in Giverny, northern France. He was to live there for the rest of his life.

He spent time painting various series that portrayed a single subject in different lighting conditions, the most famous of which was the water-lilies from his own garden. This series includes some of his most famous paintings (see page 79).

LATER YEARS

Monet felt limited by the perceived constraints of Impressionism and, towards the turn of the century, tended to paint the same scenes multiple times at different times of day. Examples include the Houses of Parliament in London, the Doges Palace in Venice and water-lilies.

He continued to work in Giverny until his death in 1926, although he suffered from failing eyesight.

"It is by dint of observation and reflection that one makes discoveries."

CLAUDE MONET,
LETTER TO FRÉDÉRIC BAZILLE,
*PSYCHOANALYTIC PERSPECTIVES
ON ART*, 2013

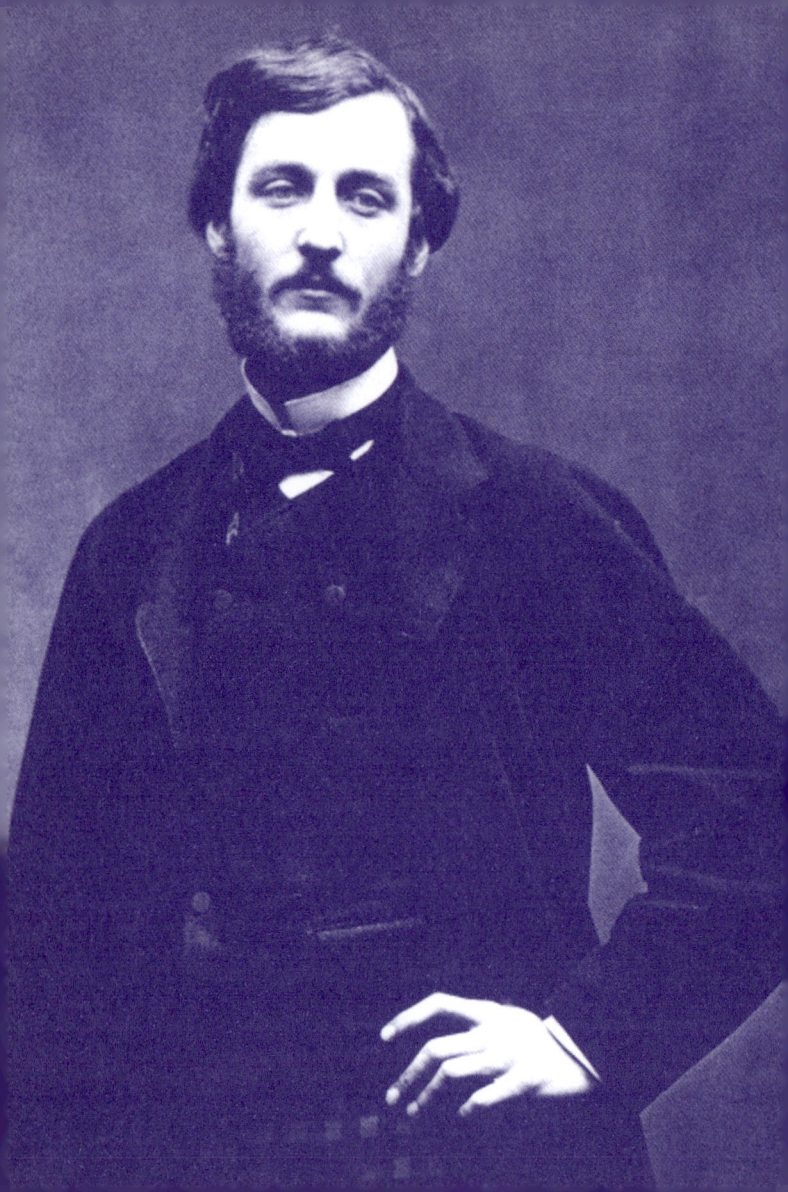

FRÉDÉRIC BAZILLE

1841–1870

Place of birth/death:

Montpellier, France/
Beaune-la-Rolande, France

Key works:

The Pink Dress (1864)
Studio on Rue Furstenberg (1865)
Family Reunion (1867–68)
View of the Village (1868)

EARLY YEARS

Frédéric Bazille was a French painter who was involved in the early development of Impressionism. Despite his tragically short career – he died in the Franco–Prussian War – the artist painted a number of works that helped lay the foundations of the movement, establishing the style.

MODEST START

Bazille was born in Montpellier in 1841 to a Protestant family. His father was a vintner; his mother was from a merchant family.

By 1862, at the age of 21, he had made his way to Paris, where he planned to pursue a career in medicine, on his father's orders. However, he had been interested in art since his youth, and while studying at medical school in the city he also began painting lessons in the studio of the well-known painter Charles Gleyre.

"I'm sure not to get killed; I have too many things to do in this life."

FRÉDÉRIC BAZILLE,
THE NEW YORK TIMES, 1992

KEY FIGURES

It was at Gleyre's studio that Bazille met what could be described as some of the most famous artists of the time: Claude Monet, Pierre-Auguste Renoir and Alfred Sisley. Together with his peers, he often worked *en plein air* (in the open air – painting outside with natural light was a key feature of the Impressionist movement) and created a number of successful paintings.

YOUNG TALENT

Most of Bazille's work is considered quite raw. The artist died young so his style does not evolve – as many of his contemporaries in the Impressionist movement. Figures in his landscapes have quite a hard-edged quality, distinguishing his style.

The painting *Studio in Rue de La Condamine* (1870), features Bazille himself, with Renoir and Manet, some other friends and a number of paintings.

"This solitude pleases me enormously; it makes me work a lot."

UNTIMELY DEATH

Bazille continued with his career as a painter and enjoyed moderate success; his most famous works were painted when he was only 23 years old – for example, *Family Reunion* and *The Pink Dress* (both 1864).

He joined the army in August 1870, fighting for France in the Franco–German War (1870–71). Bazille was shot during the Battle of Beaune-la-Rolande in November, and buried in Montpellier later that year.

THE PINK DRESS

BY FRÉDÉRIC BAZILLE, 1864

Location: Musée D'Orsay, Paris, France

This is a portrait of the artist's cousin, Therese des Hours. She is seated, and in the background is a town and some trees. It is an important piece, featuring loose brushwork, blurry details and areas of colour that hardly blend. *The Pink Dress* is an important Impressionist painting, featuring its subject *en plein air*.

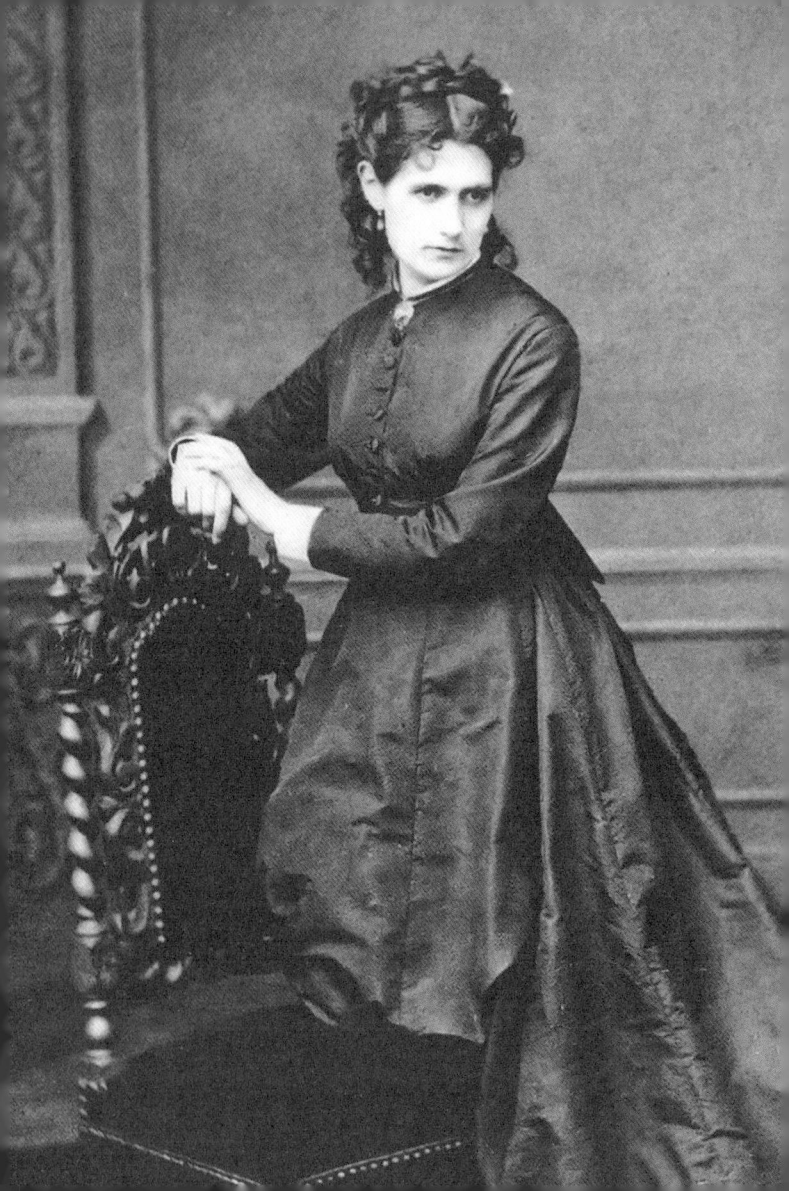

BERTHE MORISOT

1841–1895

Place of birth/death:

Bourges, France/Paris, France

Key works:

View of Paris from the Trocadero (1871–72)
The Cradle (1872)
In the Wheatfield (1875)
Young Girl in a Ball Gown (1879)

EARLY YEARS

Berthe Marie Pauline Morisot was born in Bourges in 1841 to a wealthy family. Her father was a local administrator who had studied at the prestigious École des Beaux-Arts in Paris. The family moved to the capital in 1852.

Under the tutelage of painter Joseph Guichard (1806–80), Morisot learned by copying paintings in the Louvre museum. She also studied under the plein-air landscape painter Camille Corot (1796–1875).

MORISOT AND MANET

During the 1860s, Morisot developed a close professional relationship with Manet.

In 1864 she began submitting works to the Paris Salon, where she displayed regularly through the rest of the decade. Given that she was female and only 23 when her first paintings were shown there (*Souvenirs des bords de l'Oise* and *Vieux chemin à Auvers*), this was a significant achievement.

EXHIBITION

In 1874, Morisot was invited
to exhibit with the Société
Anonyme des Artistes-Peintres,
Sculpteurs, Graveurs. This was
the landmark event that would
become known as the first
exhibition of the Impressionists.
She was the only woman to take
part in the exhibition.

MOTHER AND PAINTER

After she married Eugène, the
younger brother of Édouard Manet,
in 1874, Morisot continued her career
as a painter. They a daughter, Julie,
who was frequently the subject
of paintings by her mother, and
who was also painted by the other
Impressionists, Manet and Renoir.

STYLE

Critics often celebrated the delicacy of Morisot's work. In her early paintings, particularly watercolours, she employed a fairly restrained palette. When she moved on to oil paint and pastels, her style evolved and texture became much more prominent. By the 1880s Morisot was working much more with coloured pencils and charcoal, and drawing. Her style continued to develop throughout her fascinating career.

For subject matter, Morisot rarely painted men, preferring women and children, usually in domestic scenes in France.

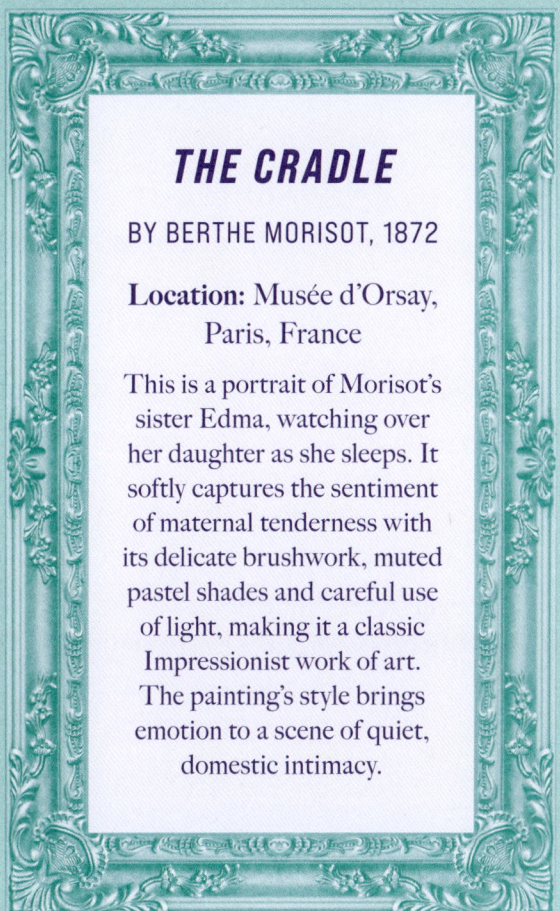

THE CRADLE

BY BERTHE MORISOT, 1872

Location: Musée d'Orsay, Paris, France

This is a portrait of Morisot's sister Edma, watching over her daughter as she sleeps. It softly captures the sentiment of maternal tenderness with its delicate brushwork, muted pastel shades and careful use of light, making it a classic Impressionist work of art. The painting's style brings emotion to a scene of quiet, domestic intimacy.

POPULARITY

Although Morisot was critically acclaimed and popular at the peak of the Impressionist era, she was subsequently not as well-known as many of her male counterparts. She has therefore often been referred to as "The forgotten Impressionist".

Morisot was one of the central, founding figures of the Impressionist movement and through her career she fought preconceptions of the role of women in society and art.

"We also consider that Miss Berthe Morisot's name and talent are too important to us to do without."

EDGAR DEGAS,
THE PRIVATE LIVES OF THE IMPRESSIONISTS BY SUE ROE, 2006

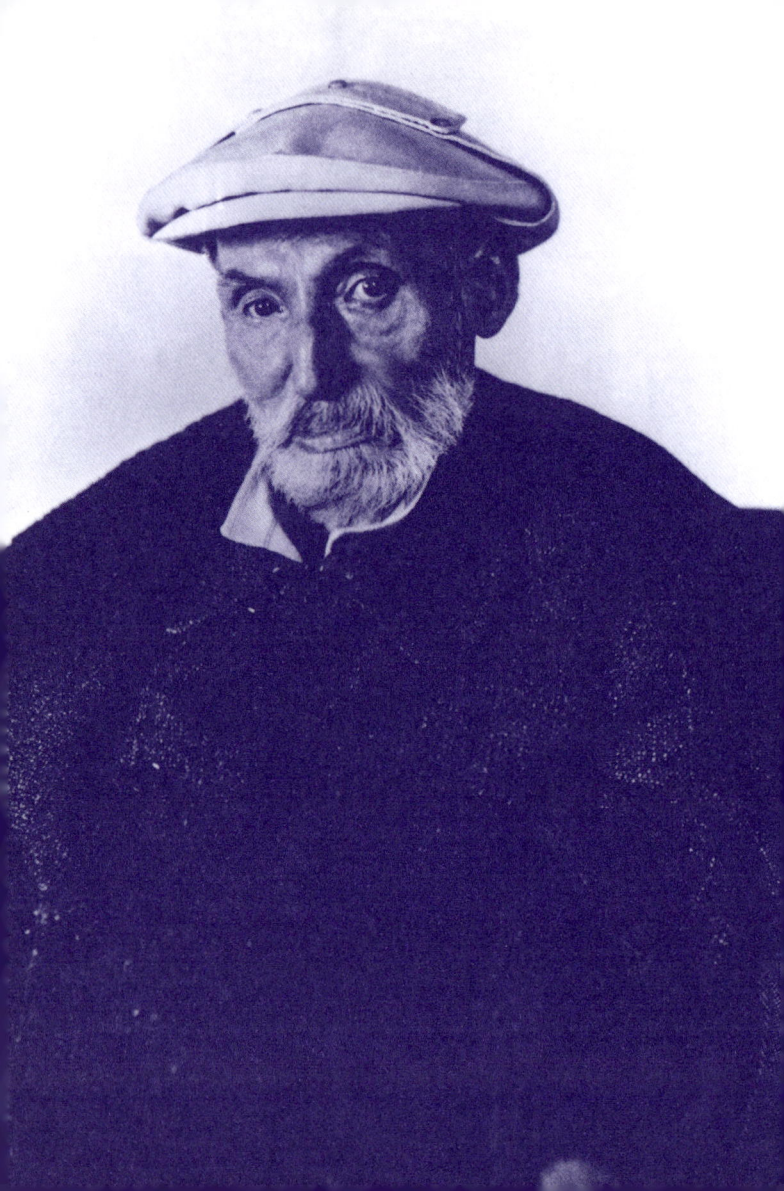

PIERRE-AUGUSTE RENOIR

1841–1919

Place of birth/death:

Limoges, France/
Cagnes-sur-Mer, France

Key works:

The Theatre Box (1874)
Bal du Moulin de la Galette (1876)
Luncheon of the Boating Party (1881)
Venice: The Doge's Palace (1881)
Young Girls at the Piano (1892)

EARLY YEARS

Pierre-Auguste Renoir was born in Limoges in 1841. Three years later the family moved to Paris. Renoir's father was a tailor and of modest means. They settled in a district not far from the Louvre museum.

The young Renoir began an apprenticeship as a painter of porcelain. He did not like the work, and preferred time spent looking at art and copying paintings in the Louvre, where he was a frequent visitor in his spare time.

POOR BUT TALENTED

Renoir's artistic prowess was recognized by the porcelain factory owner, who encouraged him to start drawing lessons. In 1862 Renoir left his job and began to study under the Swiss artist Charles Gleyre, who was also teaching the Impressionists Frédéric Bazille, Claude Monet and Alfred Sisley.

Unlike many of his contemporaries, Renoir was very poor at this time, often lacking the means to even buy basic supplies for his work.

INFLUENCES

Much of Renoir's artistic inspiration came from the Impressionists Camille Pissarro (technique and working-class subject matter) and Édouard Manet (modern life and colour).

In the early 1880s, Renoir travelled in Southern Europe and North Africa, where he encountered works by Raphael (1483–1520), Diego Velázquez (1599–1660) and Peter Paul Rubens (1577–1640). They were to influence his work after 1900, when he moved away from Impressionism, towards a more Classical style of painting.

"In working directly from nature, the painter ends up by simply aiming at an effect, and not composing the picture at all; and he soon becomes monotonous."

PIERRE-AUGUSTE RENOIR,
RENOIR: HIS LIFE AND WORK
BY FRANCOIS FOSCA, 1975

SUBJECTS MATTER

Renoir often painted groups of people, at gatherings, mealtimes or other celebrations.

He had a fondness for landscapes (some painted *en plein air*), although the female nude was the one of the most popular subjects in his work.

He also painted portraits.

BAL DU MOULIN DE LA GALETTE

BY PIERRE-AUGUSTE RENOIR, 1876

Location: Musée d'Orsay, Paris, France

This painting, in true Impressionist style, captures the fleeting joy of a Parisian night with vibrant, dappled light and loose brushwork. Renoir's style celebrates movement, humanity and the shimmering atmosphere of modern life.

STYLE

Renoir was particularly skilful with his use of colour saturation and subtlety of light. Much of his work, particularly of people, seems to almost glow with colour, in a most dramatic effect.

Renoir used the technique of broken brushstrokes to great effect, creating a sense of movement and vibrancy.

His painting style became more classical after his visits to Italy, following which he made attempts to distance himself from Impressionism.

GOOD COMPANY

When Renoir attended the studio of Charles Gleyre in 1862 to begin his formal training as an artist, he met a number of other painters, including Claude Monet and Alfred Sisley. Together they formed a core part of what would become the Impressionist movement.

Renoir sometimes worked side by side with Monet, painting the same scenery with different interpretations. Monet tended to prioritize light and colour, Renoir the beauty and sensuality of the subject.

SALON SUCCESS AND STABILITY

Renoir exhibited in the first few Impressionist exhibitions, but this did not really lead to much success for him from a financial point of view. His subsequent pieces that were shown at Le Salon, however, did lead to more financial stability, and by the 1880s Renoir was a painter of some repute and made a good living from selling his artworks in France and beyond.

"For me, a painting must be a pleasant thing, joyous and pretty – yes, pretty. There are too many unpleasant things in life for us to fabricate still more."

PIERRE-AUGUSTE RENOIR,
HISTORY OF COLOR IN PAINTING
BY FABER BIRREN, 1965

PORTRAIT OF WAGNER

During Renoir's travels abroad he met Richard Wagner (1813–1883) in Sicily. A great music lover, Renoir was an admirer of the German composer's work, and was very keen to meet him.

Wagner had just finished *Parsifal*, and as the two men got on well, Wagner agreed to sit for a portrait the next day. During a thirty-five minute sitting, Renoir painted an interesting piece, with a multi-coloured background that contrasts with the composer's dark clothing and brooding expression.

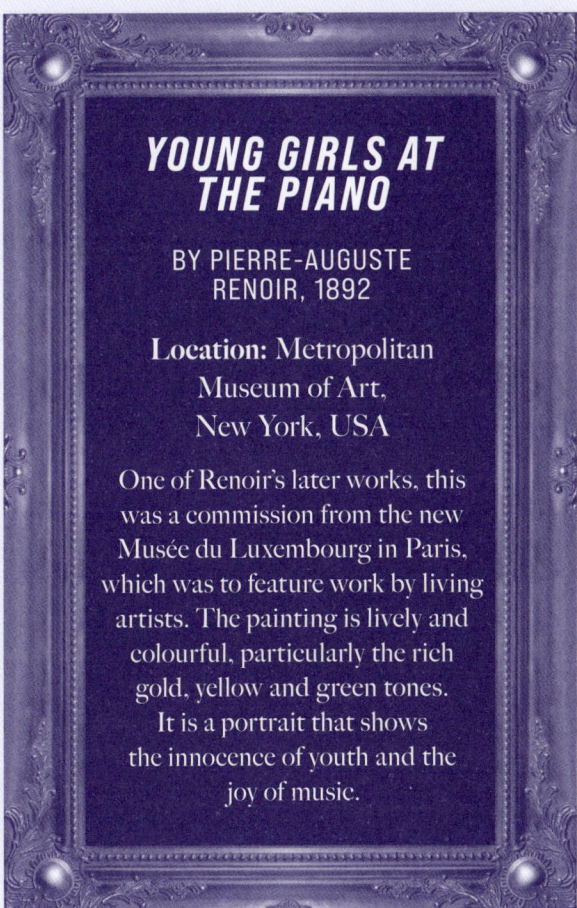

YOUNG GIRLS AT THE PIANO

BY PIERRE-AUGUSTE RENOIR, 1892

Location: Metropolitan Museum of Art, New York, USA

One of Renoir's later works, this was a commission from the new Musée du Luxembourg in Paris, which was to feature work by living artists. The painting is lively and colourful, particularly the rich gold, yellow and green tones. It is a portrait that shows the innocence of youth and the joy of music.

LATER LIFE

During the 1890s, Renoir began to suffer from rheumatoid arthritis, but he continued to paint. He moved away from Paris to the south of France, and settled in Cagnes-sur-Mer, near the coast.

He lived to see his paintings in the Louvre – Renoir famously visited the museum in the year of his death, 1919 – alongside those of the great masters he had admired all those years ago.

He remains one of the most popular artists of all time.

VALUABLE SALE

In 1990, Renoir's *Bal du Moulin de la Galette* (1876) sold at auction in New York for $78m to Japanese art collector Ryoei Saito. It was a smaller version of the work that hangs in the Musée d'Orsay (see page 107).

It became the most expensive Impressionist painting ever sold (at the time), as well as the most expensive work by Renoir.

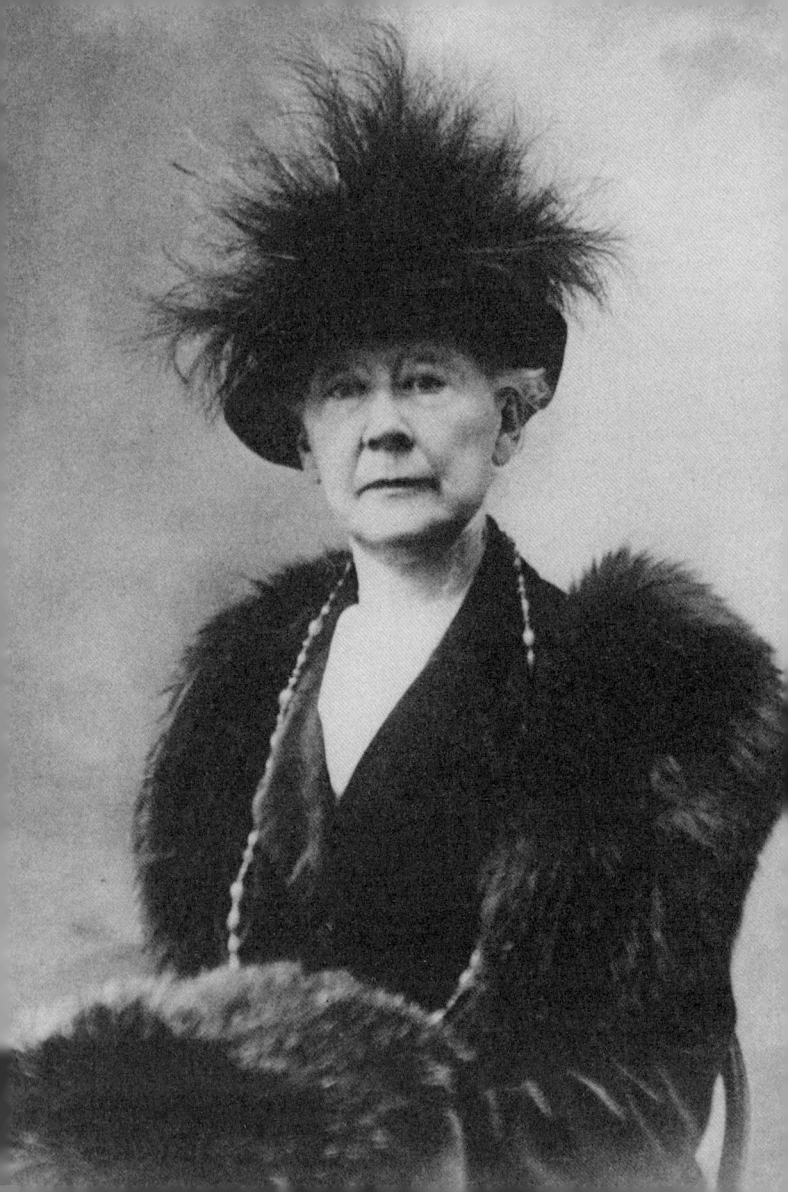

MARY CASSATT

1844–1926

Place of birth/death:

Allegheny Pennsylvania, USA/Paris, France

Key works:

In the Loge (1878)
Woman at Her Toilette (c. 1891)
The Boating Party (1893–94)
Mother and Child (c. 1905)

EARLY YEARS

Mary Stevenson Cassatt was born in 1844 in Allegheny City, which is now part of Pittsburgh, Pennsylvania, in the USA. Part of a very wealthy family, in 1865 she travelled to France to continue her artistic training.

Cassatt settled in Paris, where she studied under the artist Jean-Léon Gérôme (1824–1904).

TWO ARTISTS

Cassatt and Degas admired each other's work but did not meet until 1877, when the French artist introduced Cassatt to the other Impressionists and invited her to submit artwork. Cassatt became the only American to contribute to Impressionist exhibitions.

Cassatt worked in pastels and paint, prints and etchings. She specialized in paintings of women, usually in domestic locations, and was known for capturing a moment, in true Impressionist style.

"What one would like to leave behind one is superior art, and a hidden personality."

MARY CASSATT,
THE NEW YORK TIMES, 2024

MOTHER AND CHILD

BY MARY CASSATT, *C.* 1880

Location: Wichita Art Museum, Kansas, USA

In this striking image, a woman in a dark dress hugs a young child. It contains many essential elements for an archetypal Impressionist image: broad, wobbly strokes in the background, a surprising choice of colours and fascinating subject matter.

It is a very emotional image, rendered even more interesting by the choice of angles of the subjects, with many facial features missing.

FAMILY PORTRAIT

During the late 1870s and early 1880s, the subjects of Cassatt's works were often her family (especially her sister Lydia) portraits, and audiences at the theatre and the opera. Later she made a specialty of the mother and child theme, and it is for this that she is most famously remembered.

Mary Cassatt never married and she did not have children. All of her private letters and diaries were destroyed around the time of her death, leaving little clue as to the inner thoughts of this fascinating, mysterious artist.

MARY CASSATT

"Oh how
wild I am to
get to work,
my fingers
fairly itch!"

MARY CASSATT,
PHILADELPHIA MUSEUM OF ART, 2024

"I arrange my subject as I want it, then I go ahead and paint it, like a child."

PIERRE-AUGUSTE RENOIR,
SCRIBNER'S MAGAZINE, 1912